EVERY WRITER HAS A THOUSAND FACES

BOOKS BY DAVID BIESPIEL

POETRY
The Book of Men and Women
Wild Civility
Pilgrims & Beggars
Shattering Air

PROSE
Every Writer Has a Thousand Faces

EDITIONS
Long Journey: Contemporary Northwest Poets
Artists' Communities

DAVID BIESPIEL

EVERY WRITER HAS A THOUSAND FACES

FOR WRITERS, ARTISTS, MUSICIANS,
DANCERS, AND ANYONE ELSE WHO
LEADS A CREATIVE LIFE

PORTLAND,
OREGON

Published by KELSON BOOKS
2033 SE Lincoln, Portland, Oregon 97214
kelsonbooks@gmail.com

Library of Congress Control Number: 2010930760

Images of Dangos (Chapter 5) courtesy of Jun Kaneko.
Images of drawings (Chapters 6 and 7) courtesy of Philip Sylvester.
Book and cover design by Garth Weber
Cover art by Philip Sylvester

ISBN 978-0-9827838-0-1

Printed in the United States of America.

Kelson Books are printed on paper from certified
sustainable forestry practices.

FOR MY SON

Preface

If you only read one sentence in this book I hope it's this one: A lot of the time just sticking with it is what this whole business of writing, making art, playing music, making songs, performing, and living a creative life is all about.

I've been a faithful adherent to that idea for over twenty years, and during that time one particular experience still inspires me. When I was a Stegner Fellow at Stanford University in the 1990s, the social activist and poet Adrienne Rich paid a visit to our workshop. Rich, who had just retired from teaching literature and women's studies at Stanford, was famous for spending as little time as she could with the creative writing fellows. I always admired her for that. Some of the students were excited that she was coming that Tuesday afternoon to our weekly workshop because they hoped she would look closely at our poems and give advice earned from years in the vineyard. Praise from

Adrienne Rich, if it were to be given, would be high praise for sure.

A couple of us, however, weren't much thrilled with that prospect. Not because we didn't admire Rich—we did. Certainly I did. But we'd also grown weary of workshops in general. It doesn't take long in even a decent writing workshop for a writer to know without any doubt what each person is going to say about a new poem or story. Any workshop can devolve into a set piece: One person speaks about how the writing under review made her feel, another person speaks about this or that detail being earned or un-earned, and still another person compares the writing to something he's read and if the writing was more like that it'd be great ("some three-eyed monkeys would be good on page three!"). Was it Gertrude Stein who once said, "A workshop is a workshop is a workshop?"

This is not to denigrate all writing workshops, of course. Some are spectacularly inspirational. But it's important for everyone in a workshop to remain focused on why you're there. To my mind, you go into writing workshops to broaden your self-understanding of how you work on your writing and on what you value in writing. If an individual story or poem gets improved, that's a bonus. A good workshop is one that focuses on the making of writing.

That's what I was hoping for, I think, that early spring afternoon in

1994 when Adrienne Rich returned to Stanford to meet with the Stegner Fellows. I just wanted to listen to Adrienne Rich talk. I didn't much care what she wanted to talk about either. I admired her because I liked that she'd done more as a poet than only write poems. She exemplified a literary life as a private poet whose body of poetry had evolved in interesting ways for forty years and as public poet, a citizen-poet, who spoke forcefully in the arena of civic engagement and political life. I always liked that about Adrienne Rich. I liked that Rich's great lesson to a writer is this: writing requires solitude but life doesn't.

Adrienne Rich is petite. She speaks with the accent from her Baltimore childhood. She barely made it up to the edge of the round table that we were gathered around in the Jones Room in Building 50 on the Stanford campus. The Jones Room was a dingy lounge with overstuffed armchairs and couches and the small, crusty seminar table. The walls were cinder-block chic. Hanging on the walls were portraits of members of the Jones family that had donated money to Stanford to support creative writing lectureships and also, I guess, this charmingly seedy room used weekly for workshops by the Stegner Fellows.

Fortunately, Rich didn't much want to run a standard workshop at all and quickly dispensed with the toil of it. She said she wanted to ask us one question and let our conversation grow from there. There was some uncomfortable shifting around in chairs from some of my fellow students at this unexpected turn. One woman, I remember, forcefully stuffed the copies of her poems into her bag and all but slammed her notebook down in dismay.

"Are you in it for the long haul?" Rich asked, emphasizing the *o* in "long."

I sat up in my chair, delighted. What an open-ended question, for one thing, and a pertinent one.

Certainly I'd known it before Adrienne Rich showed up that day, but that moment in the Jones Room at Stanford settled it for me: Workshops are not helpful if they only pick at the cat's whiskers of the piece of writing on the table. Workshops also need to address large issues in writing—whether it's "why do you write?" or "what is the importance of the expression 'once upon a time?'" or "what does it mean to tell the truth in writing?" In that tense moment at Stanford, Adrienne Rich pressed on with more important questions: "Are you present enough in your sense of your self as a writer and in your process of writing to keep at it? Do you expect to evolve and even reject your past accomplishments, even the method that you've used to write? Is a life as a writer worth it?"

And: "What skills do you need to write throughout your life?"

Now that's a workshop!

My general answer to Rich's questions is one I more or less borow from Joseph Campbell's definition of the hero. In this case the hero is the writer who receives a call out of the ordinary world. Reluctant at first, the writer receives encouragement and crosses the threshold into the fullness of the imagination where the writer encounters tests, assistants, and challenges. At the inmost portions of the cave of the writer's imagination, the writer endures a variety of ordeals, then seizes on that experience and pursues transformation of the experience by writing. Finally, the writer returns to the ordinary world with the treasure—a poem, a story, an essay, a novel. Every writer enters this heroic myth at the beginning of every creative endeavor.

That's my general answer. My specific answer also comes from Campbell's famous take on the hero—that a hero has a thousand faces because every human being must reenact the hero's journey. Every writer has a thousand faces, too. Every poem, story, painting, or choreography is an occasion to don those thousand faces through the process of making one version after another of the singular piece of art at hand.

That's a little vague, I know. There'll be more on that as I continue. But for now I want only to say that to be a creative person is one of the ongoing heroic acts of your life. And the journey to becoming a writer is worth every step. One question every writer has is this: *How do I stay on the journey consistently?*

This book is my take on how you might do just that.

1.

Everything I say in this book about writing or about living with creativity at the center of your life is meant to give you, at most, a fresh way of thinking. Because I'll be speaking about the art and process of writing, and then mostly about writing poems because that's what I write, I plan to use poetry as the central motif for the book. But please feel free to read "writer" or "poetry" as just a functioning metaphor—whether you're a prose writer, a painter, drawer, dancer, sculptor, musician, or a person with creative interests outside of the arts. If you're looking for ways to stimulate your creative life, you'll find ideas about the incubatory process here.

However I would be dishonest if I didn't say that perhaps nothing in here will work for you. Everything I write in this book about creativity may simply just apply to me and me alone. I'm going to convey it with a lot of certainty. I'm going to say it as if it might save your life. But some years ago I was doing something different in my habits and some years from now I might be doing something else. I present myself as a model. I present this method as a successful strategy developed over time in the writers' workshop at the Attic. But perhaps it's not going to be exactly the model or method for you. Nonetheless, there's a good chance that the gestalt of this book, its general thrust and suggestions, are going to help you appreciate something more about your own creative habits and stimulate you to think more inventively about your creative endeavors, your creative journeys, and your imaginative life.

My take on creativity in general and on the understanding I have about my own compositional habits in particular have always been largely intuitive and not intellectualized, more of the body than of the mind. There's a tactile sense when I write. I hear words as *things*, smell them, touch them, see them as physical shapes—the letters of the alphabet especially. They have a heft and presence for me. Then, other times I just go on faith. It's not an exaggeration to say that whenever I try to share my ideas about creativity using some sort of received intellectual framework, I feel like that elephant that was caught on stage at Carnegie Hall, dressed in a tutu and playing the piano, who was overheard muttering, "My god, what I am I doing here? I'm a flutist, for crying out loud."

So I'm not going to be overly technical, not going to use avant garde, traditional, or state-of-the-art critical vocabulary. Because here's the thing: My answer to Adrienne Rich's questions is that the way to stick with it over the long haul is to fail and fail again. That's what I mean by a thousand faces. To create is to re-create.

So, I encourage you to fail. I don't mean, as the cliché goes, risking failure. I mean I want to encourage you actually to fail. I want you to have faith in not just the idea but also the ideal that failing is the engine of your creative endeavors. I know this sounds like a platitude. Hang in there with me. Later I'll show you how failing has pragmatic value and practical applications in writing and making art. There are many books about what happens to you *after* you begin writing, composing, drawing, painting, or day-dreaming. I want to talk to you about your experience as an artist prior to that point and before you begin doing any of those things. My interest is in the ways that you generate material. How you edit, revise, revamp, perfect, or polish is a subject for another book.

As I say, because I write poems I'll be using the writing of poems as my governing model. Because I teach writing, this book is naturally suited to writers. I'll be talking about making art or performance in a general sense, but I'll be talking about writing more specifically, especially at the level of the writing medium—*words*—and about using that medium the way painters use light and color, musicians use instruments and notes, and sculptors clay and water and fire. This book is about accessing those materials prior to the point of creation.

My bedrock principle as it has evolved in my life as a writer is this: Put off the first draft for as long as possible.

Now you may call that procrastination or you may call it laziness. I prefer to glorify it by calling it *indolence*. But it's my method—to put off the first draft for as long as possible. My advice to you is to not make the first draft, to not start it, and to not give in to the impulse to write or paint or sculpt or choreograph or dance. My advice is to put off starting every new piece—because as soon as you make the first draft, a certain end is in sight and it may not be the end you want.

Let me focus on writing. I define a first draft as a compositional action determined to find completion. Even if the narrative or expressive end in that first draft is not immediately in sight for you, you're in sight for it. You may not see what your options are at the beginning, but your options coalesce and harden even in your first few sentences. As soon as you write down this thing or that thing—something like, "My father had his near-fatal stroke in the final lap of his daily three mile run in 1976"—doors and windows of perception and possibility start opening and closing faster than you can say, "What?! What? What was that I just wrote?" With that one sentence, the story is in motion, the poem is out of the gate, and the essay is down the block. The doors and windows of perception that have opened draw you toward them, and the ones that close are damned hard to open again. When you look at the concept of a "draft" this way, a "revision" of that "draft" becomes a sequence of compositional reactions geared toward fulfilling the ambitions of the initial draft.

So I believe it's best to avoid making a first draft. Don't do it. Don't write the first draft. That's my advice. If you're intrigued, keep reading. If not, I'm sorry you wasted your money.

Now throughout this book I'm going to describe my own journey as a writer from first draft believer to first draft avoider and how not writing a first draft improved the spirit of my imagination. When I first began organizing my adult life around being a writer, I was in my twenties, living in a small town of 42 people in a remote village in southern Vermont. In those days I had total faith in the tried-and-true method of writing a first draft and then proceeding into a repeated sequence of revising it. That's the draft-and-revise method. Or, I should say, I didn't have total faith. I just didn't know any other way of doing it. Here's what I'd do: I'd sit down and write a draft of a poem. Then I'd revise it again and again in order to figure out what I was actually trying to say. I'd write something and then to try to fix it. I'd ask myself, "How do I fix this?" Does this sound familiar to you? All along I was trying to steer these drafts—via revision—into a final poem.

I wrote the poems in my first book, *Shattering Air,* this way. I believed that through my method of draft-and-revise I was trying to do three things. Get the observation right. Understand and interpret the psychic correspondences between myself and the observed. And last, fulfill something I understood from a quotation I'd fallen in love with by the German mystic, Jacob Boeheme, "We are all asleep in the outward man." Obviously in order to have even a small amount of success, I had to get that understanding and interpreting part right. That's what draft-and-revise demands of a writer. I had to know what *this* was and what *that* was, what *here* was and what *now* was, what the *present* was and what the *past* was, what the *observed* was and what *I* was. A pretty tall order, and sometimes I got lucky.

I'll give you an example. Here's a poem from *Shattering Air*. The announced subject revolves around two divers (as in the Olympic sport of diving). Two teenaged divers have snuck up onto the top platform of a diving tower, 33 feet above the surface of the pool, to have some petting and romance. The unannounced subject in the poem is the ever-present fleeting mixture of pleasure and despair. What you need to know about me is that from age seven until 22 I competed as a diver. I was a national and collegiate diver, competed against the legendary Greg Louganis, and later in life I developed and coached international and national champions and finalists. I say this because I'm going to talk about diving later but also to contextualize this poem:

TOWER

Fifteen years old and naked, quivering,
Stomachs flat on the ten-meter platform
Of a strange pool, 3 o'clock in the morning,
Bonnie Horton and I leaned our heads over
The hard edge of the tower to make out
The liquid surface below us, four arms
Hanging limp, loose, in the 90-degree
Darkness, swaying, knocking each other,
Playfully pulling a wrist hard enough
So one of us would fall into the flat
Blue hole of relief. I kept looking
For the water's wind-ripple, but so dark,
We could barely see the starting blocks

Or the deck chairs. And I could hardly see

The fence we'd snuck over, to climb up, strip

For the first time together, kiss, and touch

Helplessly, hysterically, Bonnie's two

Gold bracelets jingling like laughter,

Not a care but to hold her body

As close to mine as she'd allow,

To reverse-somersault down finally

To cool off. I never wanted to leave

That tower, never wanted to let go

Of a moment that lucky, but suddenly,

In the play and tug, one of her bracelets

Broke—I tried to watch it plummet,

See the splash, jump down to get it.

I couldn't. It bounced. Clink-clink.

Clink. On the concrete bottom of the well.

We lay there, disordered,

The air rough and shattering, distance

Clenched in our lungs like a giant fist,

The heat lingering. Bonnie said, O, or cried,

Softly, I don't remember. Amazed,

I was looking at my hands, and I still wonder
How they could hold pleasure one minute, close
To the lips, touching, wet. Skinless wind
The next. The veins throbbing over the cold depths
As they would the next morning at ten-meter
Workout, at our pool, before my first dive,
A front-one-and-one-half with a full twist,
My body tearing the sky, the cool water
Pure, fragrant, taking me whole.

"Tower" is based on a true story. The way I report it in the poem is the way it happened. Two teenage kids climb an abandoned diving tower on a foggy night and take off their clothes. They fool around on the platform of the tower completely unaware—because of the fog—that the water has been drained from the pool. Then, when the girl's bracelet breaks, they realize the mortal danger they're in—both on the tower and also in the realm of love and, by extension, life.

I wrote a draft of "Tower" in the late 1980s. I remember how important it was for me to construct the narrative to enhance the argument that life is unpredictable, dangerous, and yet also always sensual—and so I revised "Tower" in the direction of that understanding and interpretation. I wrote a draft and I worked on revising it. I did it over and over again. The process was like the instructions for washing your hair: Rinse and repeat, rinse and repeat. I don't remember how many drafts the poem went through but I'm sure it was several dozen. I remember showing it to my teachers at the time, and to my peers, and they gave me advice about fixing it that I took. The advice must have helped, as must have the method of draft-and-revise. Because, in the early 1990s, I published the poem in a magazine and then included it in *Shattering Air* where it remains, based on feedback I get, one of the more popular poems in that book.

But I have to confess I never found the draft-and-revise method pleasurable. Writing in that fashion either worked or it was a painful failure. Failures I discarded. Even if a poem like "Tower" worked in the conventional sense by being finished and published, I still had to move on to the next poem—as we all do no matter what method we use or art we make. But I never "risked failure" in writing "Tower" or on any poem from that period. I fixed problems. I solved complications. I puzzled out confusions. The thing is, even when I thought I was "risk-ing failure," I simply abandoned the drafts that didn't work and never returned to the poem. Because of that avoidance I seldom entered a new or previously undiscovered place in my imagination where failure might thrive.

I mean, I never tried to turn ash back into fire. I held to the notion of a single face, not a thousand, and simply tried to powder and doll up that face.

Look at all your abandoned drafts, and you'll know what I'm talking about. If I couldn't pretty up the poem into a final draft, I'd let it go. I certainly never risked failing anything once I had a handle on how a poem might succeed. Back then, while I knew writing is an act of imagination that includes composing a set of images, ideas, sensations, thoughts, and emotions into a new reality, I was seldom un-tethered from the old reality, especially memory, and I hadn't yet discovered how to open up my imagination so that it could receive and interpret and disseminate discovered material.

Draft-and-revise led me to focus and hone. What I was missing was a method that allowed me to blur and get lost in a contained sort of writing reverie. And yet: Even then I understood, in at least some gauzy way, that what I had to have in order to keep writing for years to come was something like a *lack* of control over my imagination, not just opening up to it. I had to find a place for noodling in my writing, not just fixing my writing. But I was a control-freak writer back then. The control over a poem that the draft-and-revise method gave me was bringing me a little success. Giving up control? That could bring, you know, a lot of failure!

Beginning in 2001, several experiences over a number of years led me to alter the way I composed poems and led me into a method of *losing control* as a means to discover material. One event had to do with drawing, another with writing a sequence of sonnets, another with looking at the sculptures of the artist Jun Kaneko, and finally another with sitting as a model for the artist Philip Sylvester.

These four experiences, along with a period of writing at a breakneck pace, shattered my preconceptions about writing and unthreaded a good deal of my orthodoxy about creativity.

2.

In early 2001 I took a drawing class from the artist Philip Sylvester. I did it during a period in which I knew I wouldn't have time to write much and wanted to do some cross training in order to keep alert to my imagination and compositional habits without actually writing. On Saturday mornings for half a year, I headed over to Phil's studio on Division Street in Southeast Portland and tried to draw photographs of faces and the occasional life study. I have to say, before I launch into this, I don't know anything about drawing and tend to do it only in snatches. I find it relaxing. That's about it.

What I was struck by immediately was that in a large warehouse-sized room of about 30 people I could see all the other students drawing on their white, butcher-block paper clipped onto the large paint-stained easels. And—here's the part I wasn't used to—obviously they could see me drawing, too. In fact, Phil encouraged us to wander around and do just that. Watch each other draw. You can imagine that as a writer who is used to working alone and who believes that solitude is essential to the growth of one's imagination I was thrown out of my element. One of the artists who attracted my attention was a retired gentleman who was a meticulous draftsman. We often worked side by side. I admired how he kept his charcoal in a neat hand-made wooden box and how he would never stoop to do anything so déclassé as to get chalk on his clothing when he was drawing. If you've ever worked with charcoal, you know that that's an amazing achievement all by itself. He approached his drawings with an intimidating aura of precision, and I used to imagine him in a previous life to be a landscaper who cut his coiffed lawn with a pair of tweezers.

Not me. By the time the hour was up, I was filthy. From the tip of my nose to the bottom of my boots, I was covered in black dust. I was, if nothing else, Pigpen as Artiste. Unlike my drawing neighbor who kept his drawing tools so orderly, I kept my pencils and chalk in a half-torn plastic bag slipped off from some morning's newspaper. I was constantly plunging my arm elbow deep into the long blue bag to fish out the right piece of chipped charcoal. Where my neighbor would painstakingly sketch and mark and cut and, you know, *draw*, I would attack the paper with gigantic swaths, smear away with the flat of my hand, get annoyed, start over, begin in one place, abandon, pick up somewhere else, cross out, cross-hatch, cuss. The contrast between the two of us was a contrast between civilized man and brute beast. But I no more could have worked in his Brahmin-like method than he could have in my peasant-odored one. In my mind, I saw him as a master draftsman. I, meanwhile, was like a dog in mud.

Mind you that what I saw and what the gentleman next to me saw—and what we drew from—were the same things. But his marks and mine were wildly opposite. His drawings were representational, while mine were expressionistic. When he drew a woman's face, it looked like a woman's face. When I drew a woman's face, it looked like the emotion "Anxiety" blasted onto something resembling a woman's face but only if you stood back 25 feet and then only if you looked at it through one eye while at the same time holding an index card in your other hand with the word "Woman" on it. My habits of wipe-and-smudge must have seemed bizarre to him who worked so delicately. He'd lay down a mark, draft, and then fix it neatly. I was all unfixed markings.

Recognizing our differences, however, was not debilitating. On the contrary, it was freeing. It made me understand something about my impulses and instincts as a creative person, something I was trying to understand in my writing studio but hadn't yet. Because at the same time I was finishing my period of flailing around in Phil's drawing studio like a dervish on a low dose, I was also beginning to write a long sonnet series—real pipe and ascot stuff—that required meticulous precision. A sequence of sonnets is one of the more painstaking endeavors a poet can attempt. Not just the fourteen-line limit for each poem but the way in which each sonnet joins and separates from the others makes writing sonnets intricate and wonderfully difficult to pull off.

In addition, I wanted to accomplish something I wasn't sure how to achieve. I wanted the language in the sonnets to sound distinctly American. I was resisting ramrod, stiff upper-lipped British sort of language for a slangy U.S. Grade-A stars and stripes brand of language. The sonnet seemed like an interesting vessel in which to investigate this established tension between Americanized street sounds and British sonnet-ized sense.

The problem was that the sonnets—and I'll try to put this accurately and employ, if you'll indulge me, some technical critical vocabulary—the sonnets sucked. Big time. My crappy sonnets prevented any room for my real goal—which was an impossible goal and why I was interested in it—of writing with an aestheticized American idiom.

I say aestheticized because no matter how natural sounding a piece of writing is, it's always only just an approximation of anything that we might label natural. Same holds for art, music, and dance. Leaves growing on trees are natural but a painting of leaves growing on trees is representational. It's the real as *depicted*, as artifice. Even at its most natural looking, all writing and all art is a re-construction. For instance, the sonnet's hey day in Britain occurred during the Renaissance. Do you think that's how people spoke in 17th century England—as they do in Renaissance sonnets? No. Renaissance metrical writing is aestheticized British speech of the Renaissance era. In my sonnet project, I wanted to gin up an aestheticized 21st century American speech within the limitations of the traditional sonnet. I wanted old-fashioned sonnets that swelled with the vast whomp and wah-wah erudition of American speech.

But I digress.

The sonnets. They weren't very good. But rather than blame myself, I decided to blame the form. And once I blamed the form and not myself, I decided, somewhat arbitrarily, to throw the traditional sonnet an elbow. I decided—as in my drawings—instead of precisely composing inside the sonnet's prescribed zone, I would smear out the lines and over-texture-ize the diction (an example of one of these sonnets comes in Part Three). Most important, I decided to overtly fail at making sonnets—and then build something new from that obvious failure. That decision—to be honest, it was more a discovery than a decision—made a big difference.

I was still composing, however, in my old way: draft, then revise, in order to fix. But when I altered the sonnet—by pushing and smearing the lines horizontally across the page and making them longer than the traditional ten syllable length of a sonnet—I noticed that the lines got more interesting as they got closer to American idioms. And here I want to be clear: The lines got more interesting to me. In fact, at this point in disrupting the traditional sonnet's line, I began making nine-line versions of sonnets instead of traditional fourteen-line sonnets. But, as I say, my only ambition at this point was just to entertain myself and see what came of it.

Then I recognized that the only way for me to get close to that American-ness in the language that I was after was to change the way I made the poems, too. Through my crazy new sonnet form, as you'll hear in a moment, I found myself reinventing the way I composed poems entirely. Through that reinvention, I discovered a way to re-invest in my experience and living imagination. It was as if I had embarked on a journey to discover thousands of new faces for my writing—both intrinsically and extrinsically. The result was an unveiling of my unconscious and imaginative mind.

3.

So what did I do? What was my new method? I stopped trying to write the "first draft" altogether and instead I just tinkered with words prior to composing anything. This is when I began to avoid writing the first draft. I used this word-tinkering, or word-list, or what I came to call word-palette method for every poem that came after. Every poem in my new series of "sonnets" was started the same way using the same method—as I'll show you in a moment. By fixing my method of writing to begin always with just tinkering before I did anything else *and* also deciding to work in just one form (my nine-line sonnet), I created room for myself to focus exclusively on language. I called this stretched-out sonnet an "American Sonnet" because the term kept me tethered between the old-fashioned sonnet that I had failed to write and what I discovered out of that failure, my newfangled, so-called American Sonnet.

Before I get to that, I want to say a similar sort of prep work takes place in other artistic endeavors, too. The dancer does bar work, the actor improvisational games, the sculptor stretches clay, the painter mixes paint, the businessman makes lists, and so on. In that moment of focusing on prep work for my writing, I was both giving up and gaining something that let my imagination uncork itself from, well, myself.

Here's one of the American sonnets, "Epileptic." The poem is a metaphor for what I've been describing. It characterizes the seizure that fills an artist when he is lost in the reverie of creation. "Epileptic" is not a traditional sonnet, but one of my invented American Sonnets:

EPILEPTIC

Always there'd be the stoic necessity that sucked the troubles dry,
  and, maybe, baking in the brain
Like a harlequin, a quarrel good enough a sign for blood to
  cradle through the hours and save me from the spell
Of swallowing the tongue. How brawny, errant I'd be. The
  episode a requiem (like an insect's stinging sliver
It seized my sleeping neck). Then all at once a noiseless gush, a
  splicing blurt of charm—though charm's not what it was—

Gauze of nerves, dizzy stroke, a jigging operative kowtow, the
    eyes like craggy currants,
The body seized by heart and throat like telling someone you're
    in love you know can never love you back.
A needle in the eye—my prayer to puncture and destroy the
    curse.
Sometimes it's hard to know what's worse, the way convulsions
    tear the tongue or these minutes in between

One madness and another—the sunny, dust-impending stir,
    the icy air and everywhere-awaiting fear.

In giving up on the traditional sonnet and then inventing a version of the sonnet—something new *in the sonnet family*, something with a different sonnet face—I also gave up, in the early part of making a poem at least, on a draft-and-revise compositional work-habit. My new habit would be one I call method-and-versions. It's not the only method I use, it's not a silver bullet, and you shouldn't think I'm suggesting it's *the way* to write. It simply helped me to re-conceive how I compose. It helped me learn to move laterally in my consciousness and imagination.

You can get a sense of my understanding of all this from the 2003 introduction to my book of American Sonnets, *Wild Civility*:

The poems in this collection represent two years of writing al-most exclusively in a single form. The form is my own variation on the sonnet, a nine-line sonnet, what I've come to call an "American sonnet."

The prototypical line for these nine-liners is decametric (though as free verse variations, the lines vary, some more & others less than ten metrical feet). These sonnets are shorter than their English counterpart by lineation, nine lines versus fourteen lines, but longer by sound, one hundred & eighty syl-lables versus one hundred & forty syllables.

Regarding the speakers of the poems: Imagine a Coke bottle, shattered & whole. If the whole bottle represents a single unified voice (my voice, say, my core lyric voice), then the shards of glass are fractions of that single voice. In this sense, the speaker's dra-matic voice in each poem represents a fragment of my voice—a lyric fragment, that is, that gets just nine lines to speak.

To my surprise, the result has been a kind of explosion of language. I've drawn from the vocabularies of history, science, art, sport, philosophy, religion, literature, government, domestic life, etc.—often within the same poem & in varying registers of language.

I've come to imagine the nine-line sonnet to be like one of those classic Thunderbirds, something distinctly American: wide, roomy, & with a robust engine.

But to get to that new poem, as I say, I changed the way I worked. Here's what happened: Because my form was fixed, I was able to play with the medium itself—just seeing words as natural materials—prior even to starting on a poem. Instead of sitting down to write and see what happens as in the draft-and-revise method, I began simply by making my word-palettes. Then, from these word-palettes, I began to find a path toward meaning, drama, and narrative. Here's a sample of one word-palette with a few proverbs and pithy sayings thrown in at the end:

stag horn	*hostage*	*throng*
maple leaf	*leopard spots*	*flames*
golden goal	*gurgle*	*angle/dog*
swill	*swallows*	*wish*
backsplash	*shebang*	*kasbah*

umpteen	*putter*	*punish*
bird-dog	*grates*	*brogue*
ramshackle	*karma*	*chalk*
four square	*scuff*	*aqueous*
beau gest	*post haste*	*subject*
salad days	*lads*	*sadly*
shenanigan	*gassy*	*hag*

Have patience awhile; slanders are not long-lived. Truth is the child of time; erelong she shall appear to vindicate thee.
~ Immanuel Kant

I dance to the tune that is played.
~ Proverb, (Spanish)

Therefore the ungodly shall not stand in the judgment, nor sinners in the congregation of the righteous.
~ (Psalm 1v5) KJV

I'm sure this list just looks like a bunch of craziness! But if you were to try this a few times, you might discover that the lists are highly suggestive, allusive, and alluring. They provide an avenue to the psyche by allowing your imagination to make lateral, associative, expressionistic connections. The word-palette (or, depending on the kind of writing you do, idea-palette, character-palette, sketch-palette) can give you a chance to mull your subject, even to invent the subject, to concoct a subject, so that invention and memory, experience and discovery, curiosity and certainty all percolate inside your imagination prior to writing even one line or sentence.

For those of you who don't write poems and don't feel that a mere word list is transferable to what you write, then I recommend assessing your methods in order to ask yourself, what kind of preparatory palette might work? Character sketch after character sketch for the fiction writer? Scene after scene sketch for the short story writer?

Choreographer Twyla Tharp calls this sort of approach "scratching." She says, "the first steps of a creative act are like groping in the dark: random and chaotic, feverish and fearful, a lot of busy-ness with no apparent or definable end in sight…For me, these moments are not pretty. I look like a desperate woman, tortured by the simple message thumping away in my head: 'you need an idea.'" Another choreographer, Merce Cunningham, used to "cut up" dance movements from a sequence, switch them around in a random order, then ask his dancers to do the puzzle piece in that random fashion. He learned a lot about what he didn't know he needed to know. And he invented some new figurations and connections by letting go of his conscious self and adopting a happy-accident methodology during his pre-compositional, "dance-palette" preparation.

Whatever method you use, certainly it'll put a serious delay on the writing of the first draft. But that's what you want. By the time you get there, you'll know a good deal more about your subject prior to that first draft. At the same time, this sort of sketching or "scratching" or cutting up keeps you primed to be open to further discovery.

You can see that, in my use of sketching, the word-palette is essentially indiscriminate words, side-by-side words, that sound similar. The connector is the writer. What I might see in the list and what you might see are necessarily different. Moreover, what I might see working with the list on the first day of the month and what I might see working with the list on the last day of the month are necessarily different, too. So I came to trust that the "mistaken" first day reading and writing was seeding my "mistaken" last day. One failure led to another.

Here's one version of a poem that came from the list above (I made this list some years after I published the nine-line sonnets):

TO CARMIN FROM MARKET STREET

Dear Jim: The men seem less modern than they used to be.

It's as if their politesse has settled down with decent sleep

And their numerology has gone limp—

Or it's a glimmer of old glory,

Ungenerous as un-remarking about love.

Not as if that's the golden goal

But the old dogs gurgle on the corners of this city's streets,

And the faded frat boys swill the umpteenth beer

Before dark putters in like a sad punishment.

So much for the salad days, the lads seem to say,

What with the shenanigans gone gassy, and the love for hags

More an adoration for beau geste.

But these men are lovely, four-square, and post-haste.

Somewhere in a book I once meant to read

The philosopher says, "Have patience awhile; slanders are not
*   long-lived."*

I've been getting these nerves under control, sure,

But once I wanted to be chained to the divine like a hero.

Who wouldn't dance to that tune?

Even that's blistered, tugged at, less vital.

Today, in this sudden crawling rain of summer,
I can fess up to you but can't quell the lackadaisical:
Work's to be done.
Though the future's gotten fetching—
Mistrialed, unpunished, a little weary.
Once, downtown, near here, you said something about
*   godly relics*
That must be looked for on washed-out roads,
And I thought of how the ungodly don't stand in judgment,
Or sinners don't, on any road.
That's got to be from Psalms.
But the roads don't go there.
What with the flames of the maple leafs spotting the sky,
And the public square mustachioed and not so trim.
The whole fretwork of the city
Extends before me with the quadrants slipping into erasures
*   of light.*
I see this city now as a child sees a mother.
And my long-lost Texas with its tall hat
Is now more like a godfather.
See you soon, Jim.

I'll keep the gin and the limes ready,
And you can swear about the fate of old books
And good-time congregations of the righteous.
Yours, with the old genuflection. D.

As you can see from the relationship of the word-palette and this version of "To Carmin from Market Street," the individual words suggest to me an imaginative narrative. If you were to write something using the same word-palette, you would likely come up with a different narrative, one more central to your nature. In fact "nature" is the word the painter Jackson Pollack used when he responded to critics who accused his abstract expressionistic drip paintings of lacking any nature. "I'm the nature," he sniffed.

Perhaps you're still asking, is this method just for poets? The answer is no. Phil Sylvester describes a similar journey for visual artists. He says that the most important thing for you to do as a creative person is be open to what he calls "mistakes" and to be ready to break the "rules" of your habits.

On the first day of his beginning drawing classes, Phil often asks his students to draw their names over and over again. Here's how Phil puts it in his book, *Introduction to Drawing*, after he's assigned his students to draw their signatures over and over again:

Any time you notice a consistency—that is, something you do every time or a rule you unconsciously follow—I want you to break that rule or consistency. If all the signatures are neat, make some messy ones. If they are all in straight lines, start doing some in arcs and curves. If you are careful not to let any overlap, just start piling them on top of each other. Do some small, some big, some out of control, some obsessively controlled. If you can think of anything to do wrong, immediately do it. And don't stop. As long as there is more time in the exercise I want you to continue trying things. We aren't trying to arrive at a clever solution. We are trying to cram in as much experience and experimentation as the time allows.

What you are doing in this exercise is similar to what people with phobias have to do to get over the phobias. That is, they progressively expose themselves to the thing that they fear and simply notice over time that nothing happens, that they are safe and OK. It is a process of desensitization. In your case the way to get over the fears and presumptions that hold drawing back is to actively and on purpose do things that you think are wrong.

As you make these choices two things happen. Either the action you thought was inappropriate actually advances your drawing rather than holding it back or you simply find that the consequences of making so-called mistakes in drawing are insignificant. I've seen so many students, and even professional artists, hold back because they are afraid of the terrible consequences of making a mistake. What consequences? Never in my years of teaching have I seen a student injured by doing a bad drawing. I've never had a student burst into flame or lose a limb. I've never even seen a student's parents appear out of the sky and begin criticizing the student.

Look into the attitudes of people who excel at some activity. Most often you will find that those people actually embrace mistake. By not trying to hold mistakes at bay, they have the freedom to try many more things and develop an experience base far more quickly than someone who tries desperately never to fail. I once read a quote from a heart surgeon who said, "Good judgment comes from experience. Experience comes from bad judgment." Boy, if a heart surgeon can embrace that method, given the consequences he must face, certainly we can as drawers. I also once saw a poster, printed by Michael Jordan's organi-

zation, listing stats on Jordan's mistakes. He has records for things like the most shots missed in the last three seconds of an NBA game. The point of his putting out that poster was to say that when he is good, he is so incredibly good because of the experience he gained by not being afraid of making mistakes.

In other words, by throwing up air ball after air ball in your writing, you master the distinction between miss and *swish*—which because of their consonance, assonance, and rhyme these two words would fit wonderfully onto one of my word-palettes! Here's Phil again, getting his students to embrace making versions not finished products. His word for the process is "marks." He wants you to understand that the making of marks is your only certain task—just as making versions becomes the only certain task in the method I've been describing:

> *I want you to stand back from the drawing at least six to ten feet. Look at this drawing as if you just found it out on the sidewalk, as if you had nothing to do with making it. Now scan through the whole surface. Notice where there are areas that catch your interest. Don't ask why. Just notice the parts your eye is curious about, the parts your eye keeps coming back to. May-*

be it's because they are so horrible, maybe it's because they're so great or surprising. Either way, as you are noticing the parts that attract your interest, also notice the areas that your eye simply skips, the parts your eye considers non-parts of the drawing. Once you've found some of these parts that you just skip, I want you to go into those areas and try a bunch more experiments, more marking, more erasing. The idea is, many of the best parts emerged by accident. So maybe if you throw a few more accidents at the dead parts they might take off, too. Work on a dead area for a while, then move onto another. Don't obsess on an area, trying to fix it. Just give it a bunch more action then move to some other section...

Right now [while you are drawing] you are trying any old thing in the areas that don't work on your drawing. Maybe your actions will make those areas better, maybe your choices will make the areas worse, but at least the areas will change. At least they will be dislodged so some new possibilities might arise.

I believe Phil's point is this: The more you investigate change, the more you discover what you hadn't known to see. In other words, the unknown unknowns become all you confidently know. Phil continues:

What we've been doing is so characteristic of how good work gets made. If most artists were told—immediately after finishing a great piece—that they had to make another one just like it or go to jail, their response would be, "Lock me up. I don't know how I made that one so how could I make another one just like it?" Because we are always engaging problems we don't know how to solve, we are also capable of working way over our heads, achieving things we couldn't possibly achieve if we were only to take on the problems we could figure out in advance.

A number of things begin to happen when you let go like this. First, there is the freedom to look at every aspect of what you are observing, not just the ones you think you can draw or you think you should draw...Allowing drawings that are out of your control opens the door to drawing over your head. Loss of control is actually necessary if you are ever to draw what you don't already know how to draw.

I read Phil's book, *Introduction to Drawing*, years after I wrote and published the poems in *Wild Civility*. It's clear to me, though, that Phil and I share a common faith in an open, multi-faceted artistic process.

That process entails marking up my lists, dodging the first draft, fixing a title, and writing toward that title. The logistics? A single sheet of paper. I just fold my cheat sheet of paper into quarters and store it in my back pocket for a few days or weeks. Then, once I have a title for the new poem, I write the poem based on these evolving notes. I crib a version of the poem from the list of words. You might prefer a note-book—I don't think the vessel matters that much. As for what I create from the words on the list? Well, if I like what comes of it, great. If not, I move on. I pick words out of the version, start over. Make a new list, do it again. I'm not making drafts and revising to fix it. I'm making lists of words to see what resonates within me. And then thinking about how I feel about the words and the resonances.

You're asking, what connects the words? Answer: I do. Because "I'm the nature." Synonyms, homonyms, anagrams, or whatever it takes to build out the list—that's what I work with. Prose writers can similarly prepare their word-palettes prior to drafting, too. Instead of using word lists, make sketches. Let each sketch inspire the next one. And build detail sketches—what visual artists call side work—from images of other sketches. Keep at it until the needs of the story or piece of non-fiction begin to emerge in the more rational zones of your imagi-nation.

I can see now, years later, that *Wild Civility* is a book of many versions of the same impulse—to write a sonnet that sounded American and to bring my emotions to bear on the experience of that language. Thing is, though, I never wrote a sonnet. I utterly failed at writing a sonnet. I cheated the sonnet. I changed the conditions of the test that poets face when writing the sonnet. My attempt to write a sonnet series was a big, fat failure.

What came out of the failure were the poems that make up the book *Wild Civility*.

If my former method could be described as beginning with experience and moving toward language to transform that experience, then my current method is to begin with language and move toward experience, whether the experience is discovered or invented or remembered from the language on the word-palette list. The whole business is a process of unmasking the thousands of faces that inhabit those word-palettes in order to transform both language and experience into a coherent dramatic metaphor, a statement, a narrative, and if the gods are with me, a lyric poem.

4.

So the word-palette or idea-palette or sketch-palette method can become your initiating focus—and not the drafts. Then your work becomes chalking up version after version to see what comes of it. Some of my devotion now to using language or just plain words to catalyze a piece of writing, rather than initiating the process by measuring experience through memory, comes from a mild distrust I have of memory's uses to a writer. It's common to hear artists and writers ask: What is memory? How does it work? How does it impact your imagination? My answer is that when you move beyond the capacity to remember or not remember, then you very well might find yourself writing with more freedom and fluency.

In my view, one of the worst paradigms for memory, insofar as being a writer goes, is whether or not your memory is good or bad. I mean, isn't it more accurate to characterize memory not as good or bad but as simply a perspective on the facts? Because here's the thing about memory: When it comes to memory, your brain has the potential to record everything you experience. But, even if it could record *everything*, you can't always locate it. All the subtle or huge disagreements you've had with your siblings or friends, for example, about who said what or what happened when, all those times your memory lapses into a puddle of "I don't remember exactly..." that's the result of memory's fallibility. Ask any criminal lawyer or law enforcement official about the fallibility of a witness' memory, and you will be entertained with case study after case study of how memory is totally unreliable—especially if there's a gun in the room.

Memory is a sensory experience more than a factual one. Your brain takes all of your experiences and compresses them into a few essential images, emotions, and words. Then what happens is you get your current emotional feelings mixed up with what you remember. I mean, you use your present emotional framework to select what to remember from the past and to gauge how you feel about those past experiences—or, more accurately, how you now feel that you felt about those experiences.

When you recall something from your past, like a first kiss, say, you bring into your imagination the highlight and the emotion that you feel toward that experience. You also try to sense what you felt *then* (the inching forward to touch lips, the rush and blush of your heart, the courage, the vulnerability). But mostly what you sense is how you feel about it *now*. Then you generalize about the rest like the time of day, the 150 things that led to that first touch of lips, the way the air in the room seemed to go moist.

In other words, you imagine your past based on a few details and emotions (like the way you felt about the smile your beloved made right before kissing you). But so much else about the experience gets lost—because so much of your memory is connected directly to what is still essential to your interpretation of the past from the vantage point of the present. What I mean is, you interpret the past, and your interpretation becomes your memory. You *imagine* your past, not remember it. Memory isn't a replica of the past. It's your version of the past. At different moments of your life you concoct different versions of your self—or you repeat one version only to find out later that someone else has a completely different version (meaning, *memory*) of the same events.

Does it matter, then, that crucial, ongoing debate about truth and fiction? Can you fictionalize your autobiographical writing? Must you tell it exactly as it happened? These are good questions that are hard to answer fully when you realize that memory is essentially a form of fiction anyway. Being creative, being inventive, beginning with jottings of the imagination instead of experience in the compositional process—all of it uses the same part of your brain as remembering something does. So making word-palettes, for example, is creating the conditions for you to *remember forward* as it were, fashioning not the past but a future version of your memory's recreation of the past. In this sense, I would define creativity as the journey of inventing a thousand faces from a single source in order to locate the face that holds your interest the most. Inventing from the materials created in the lists of words is an act of *remembering* out of an unknowable present into a knowable and invented artistic future. Writing—like all acts of memory, like all acts of creativity—is the act of imagining a set of images and emotions into some new reality.

When I decided not to let my memory be a witness of the past and instead let my memory be a stimulant for my imagination, I opened myself up to interpreting my word-palettes as representative of my past, present, and future *all wrapped into one*. I realized, too, that most of my writing is spent not in perfecting but simply in exploring the ongoing ongoing-ness of my imaginative life. Memory isn't the essential ingredient. Repetition is. Repeating the word-palette method to discover and also rediscover what I can use as material is the key process in my writing.

Here's an example from diving again: Elite divers train six days a week, four hours a day, twice-a-day, 12 months of the year, in order to perform just ten dives at the National Championships. That's a lot of *versions* of individual dives in order to achieve success in just ten performance dives. One thing I learned at the peak of my athletic career and in my coaching career was that delaying the start of practicing helped improve both my practice and performance—though, obviously, I'd forgotten that fact when I started to write and had to relearn it.

Here's what I mean. Through much of my competitive diving career, at the beginning of practice I'd just hop onto the diving board and start doing tricks. Typically then the first twenty minutes of practice determined whether all that followed would be good or a bust. Later on I realized that the times, you know, that I actually warmed up, I practiced and performed much better, more efficiently, and more consistently. I learned that I needed to heat up my body to roughly the same place everyday—the place where I could start to dive well (read: write well).

My word-palettes are like the exact and repeated stretching and stair-running and weight-lifting I needed prior to practice or performance in diving. The word-palettes bring me to the same "heated up" place before I begin to write. Now every time I start to write, I begin with looking to achieve the same "writerly" feeling at the beginning of the effort. Whether that's a physical feeling I'm trying to re-achieve each time or one related to some interior consciousness, I couldn't say. But this repeatable feeling lets me "fail" in the warm up and "succeed" later on when it matters. I know that other writers use other methods to get heated up: reading, dancing, staring out the window, drawing, slow breathing, yoga, whatever. My warm up is making lists of words and sketching versions from those lists. Once I have something that interests me that I've taken from the many versions, only then have I arrived at my "first draft" and only then do I begin to revise in the traditional manner—to find the fixes, implement them, and then finish the work toward a polished version.

Another example, from a different discipline: The superstar hitter for the Seattle Mariners, the local baseball team in my region, is Ichiro Suzuki. He comes to the plate officially about 700 times a season. He's gotten more hits per season than any player in baseball over the last decade, about 230 hits per season. No player in modern baseball is even close to that average. Two hundred and thirty hits for every 700 times at bat—that doesn't count batting practice. And he's the best hitter in the sport! I mean, from one perspective, 230 out of 700 is atrocious. Know what I mean? Sixty to seventy percent of the time Ichiro *utterly fails* at hitting. What Ichiro Suzuki is really an expert at is failing to get a hit. He's much better at that than he is at hitting. He bats .700 in failing to hit!

If you believe you must be perfect in your writing, in your hitting, as it were, every single time you "stepped to the plate" of your keyboard, then you would quit. So forget about it. It's impossible. But if your goal is to fail and to make failure your art, you're going to arrive more consistently at a more successful space as a writer, artist, or creative person.

But isn't perfecting or polishing the writing what we're trying to do in workshop? I can hear some of you wondering. Honestly, I'm not so sure. Raymond Carver never came to terms with the changes his editor, Gordon Lish, made to his most famous stories. The published versions turned Carver into a major American short story writer. Carver believed his unpublished versions were truer to his vision.

Believe me, there's a risk in over-polishing, too. Back to diving: For a few years in the early 90s I coached one of the most talented young divers in America, a girl from Beaverton, Oregon, named Katie Case. Her athleticism combined the grace of the ballerina, the speed of a sprinter, and the agility of a half-back. She'd had some trouble with confidence and one season that trouble had reduced her amazing potential into an unimpressive puddle. It had gotten so bad she was afraid to do even a back flip, one of the sport's simplest skills. But working hard to overcome that psychological barrier the next season, she arrived at the qualifying meet for the National Championships in top form—if still a little mentally untested—and, diving-wise at least, she was ready to earn her spot for the Nationals. Fifteen years old at the time, she was performing the most difficult list of dives of any girl in her age group.

During the warm up, I sat on the pool deck next to my dear friend, Rick Schavone, the diving coach for Stanford University. When I say "dear friend" I mean, "arch nemesis whom I loved." Since I had attended Stanford, I had one ironclad rule for my divers: "I don't care what place you get in this competition so long as you beat Stanford." I was teasing Rick about my nefarious little goal when it was Katie's turn in the warm up. From the 3-meter diving board, she performed a reverse two-and-a-half somersault—a complicated inverted spinning trick that sometimes looks like the diver is spinning backwards into the diving board. For a second she was in the air, spinning like a blur, and then when she entered the water, nothing. No splash. No ripple. Just beautiful toes pointed like arrows after her body had slipped neatly, splashlessly, under the flat surface. It was breathtaking. Everyone in the natatorium gasped and then, upon her breaking the surface from under the water, burst into a roar of applause and approval. She'd smoked it all right. It definitely would have scored a few 10s. The trip to Nationals seemed like a foregone conclusion.

I was pleased. But I also thought she could have spun just *a little bit faster* if she pulled her knees closer to her chest. And if she did that, she could finish the trick higher above the water. And if she could do that, she'd score maybe a few more 10s. So I told her to do one more, and to do what I just described. Jazzed, pumped, elated, confident, she hustled back up the board, set the fulcrum, got set, marched down the board, hurtled to the tip of the board, sprang off even higher than before, pulled her knees in more tightly just as I'd asked, finished the spinning part of the trick *two feet higher* than the previous one and then, on account of that perfecting and polishing, she over-rotated so much that she landed on *top* of the water and flat on her stomach. I can't remember if she went *splat* or *thwack* or *phuwap*, but her body slammed like an ironing board on the water. Her head didn't even go under. It was like she hit the surface calm of the water and, then, just bounced a couple of times.

Again, the entire natatorium gasped. But this time, no applause, no roar, just a worried silence as a rattled Katie Case climbed slowly out of the pool.

My dear friend, Rick Schavone, turned to me and said: "I love coaching against you. You just turned a 10 into a 2."

Well, that may have been the case in the warm up. But, she knew what the "good version" felt like. So in the competition, she ratcheted down to the imperfect feeling, the "failed" feeling that worked for her earlier and hit the dive—not for 10s, but for 8s and 9s—and returned to Nationals. And not one Stanford diver beat her that day.

As with writing, it wasn't necessary for Katie to be perfect to be successful. What was necessary was sticking with it, for getting the dive that sufficed, for failing into the feeling of success.

5.

About the same time I was halfway or more into writing the poems that make up the book *Wild Civility*, I became friendly with the Japanese sculptor Jun Kaneko who has lived for many years in Omaha, Nebraska. Jun has had exhibitions and public art installations throughout the world. Much of his artwork—whether sculpted in clay, glass, or other materials—are variations and versions of his signature piece, the *dango*, which is Japanese for dumpling. Jun's *dango* is a vase-shaped sculpture with a repeated pattern painted in vivid colors or in stark black and white. Some *dangos* are small enough to fit onto the palm of your hand or on a table. Others are so large they have to be scored by lowering a ladder into the center of them, and then have to be transported on a flatbed truck.

By repeatedly sculpting *dangos*, Jun fit his vision of space and size into the versions of the same shape, the *dango*. I wouldn't want you to get the idea that you must have a signature piece or signature style in order to make art. I would say that there's an argument to be made that if you look closely at what you have created, a "signature" style is already in place. Nonetheless, an artist has just one take on the "language" of his or her art form and might spend a lifetime working to expose, explore, and enlarge that take.

DANGO 1

As you can see (*dango 1*), it's a dumpling. This one resembles a pod or a bullet. The interlocking lines form misshaped rectangles. In many of the following *dangos*, you'll see how Jun builds out his variations. None of these *dangos* are what we might call the "finished" *dango* in the way that you might think of a "finished poem" or "finished story." They all are as finished and as unfinished as the next one.

In the next *dango* (*dango 2*), the shape is similar if more squat. The lines, patterns, and colors are more complex than the first one, more varied with slants and angles.

And yet the dominant shape of the dumpling remains. In your writing you can make your versions operate the same way, too. You can have overlapping characters, scenes, lines, images, metaphors, and then build out from some of these into a new piece, a new version.

DANGO 2

What I mean is, *dango 2* does not need the other *dangos* to be a *dango*. But Jun Kaneko needs them in order to make the next one.

One of the ways to work with method-and-vision is not to repeat everything on the same scale. As in the next piece (*dango 3*), the black-and-white patterning, the rectangles and polka dots are variegated and imbalanced. In this sense, *imbalance* becomes the balance.

DANGO 3

A similar problem exists in creative writing workshops, too. For instance, when the goal of the workshop is to achieve consensus, then a writer might only be seeking balances in the poem

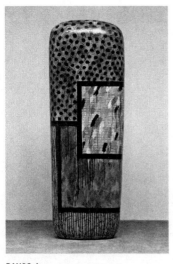
DANGO 4

or story. I can't think of anything worse for a writer than to insist on balance—or for a workshop to insist on balance either. Your writing must insist on imbalance—whether it's in texture, voice, attitude, or tone. X doesn't need to match Y.

Instead, as in *dango* 4, a little of X might mix well with a lot of Y. Or the other way around.

Notice on the following page (*dango* 5) that Jun has gone for a repeated ripple in black and white.

We've seen versions of this pattern in some of the others, but here he has added the image of a face—as if the *dango* has evolved from raw shape to a formed creature. What I like about this pairing is the reinvention within the variation. That's what a version truly is.

On page 64 is a photograph of the artist, Jun Kaneko, standing in front of one of his very large *dangos*. I've often felt that the art one makes doubles as a "self-portrait" for the artist who makes it.

You may be asking, does Jun Kaneko think he's making versions of the *dango* or something else? Once over dinner at Castagna's near

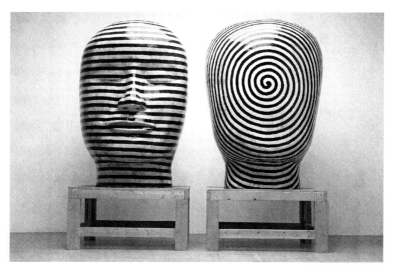

DANGO 5

Ladd's Addition in Portland during the period I was writing the American Sonnets for *Wild Civility*, Jun and I struck up a conversation about what we were both working on. He was in town for the opening of a glass exhibition of his work. I had been feeling skeptical about my new process and with the weird sonnets that came out of it. I was deeply concerned that I was essentially writing the same poem over and over again.

"No, no, no," Jun said. "None of my *dangos* are like any of the others."

"But isn't some of the criticism about them that you're just repeating yourself?" I asked.

JUN KANEKO

"The critics are wrong," he huffed, shrugging. "The *dango* still interests me. I learn something new each time I make one. I face a new problem with each one. Yes, they resemble each other. But that's because they resemble my interests. So what if they do?"

"Do you conceive of them as self-portaits then?" I asked.

"Entirely. I'm just me. I could no more make something different than become a different me."

And here I pressed him, talking about my own worries about my own poems, "But, I mean, c'mon. They are the same piece. It's another *dango* followed by another *dango*."

"Not to me. Not when I'm making them. A big one is not the same as a small one. They each live in space differently and so, for me as the maker, they are each unique. I address each as a unique problem even when they arise from the same source. And same goes for you as a member of the audience that is looking at them."

"I know for myself," I said, "that each time I make a new sonnet it's as if I've returned to the materials pile and found some semblance of the same materials, sometimes the same materials exactly. I make a new version out of what I had made before—with what I know from before."

"Yes! And this new version exists on a continuum with the others but has its own unique or perfected existence on that continuum, too. Of course, each one is a failure. That's why I must make another one. But out of that failure I learn how to make the next one. Sometimes I fear that I never succeed! But still, I keep making more *dangos*."

6.

So after all that *dango* talk took place I published the poems in *Wild Civility*. The critic David Orr in *Poetry* magazine described the explosion of language as being like a Romanian poet translating John Ashbery first into Romanian then back into English while all the while frying eggs and standing on one foot. I loved that! Then I wrote the poems that became *The Book of Men and Women*. None of these new poems were American Sonnets, but all were composed in my word-palette and multiple versions method.

When *The Book of Men and Women* was in galleys in the summer of 2009, I sat as a model for Phil Sylvester for a magazine piece I was writing for *Poetry Northwest* where I had been serving as Editor and Phil had been serving as Staff Artist. I anticipated that the sitting would be just once or twice and then he'd repair to his studio to draw the rest of it. It turned out to be twice a week for two hours for two months.

What Phil created in that time was version after version of my face, throwing dozens upon dozens of discards onto the floor of his studio or hanging them up on the wall until he came to a point of an understanding about drawing my face that provided him with, well, further understanding about drawing my face.

He wasn't going to revise to make a finished product. He was going to make versions from the same material in order to make more versions from the new material. One version of my face after another. Here's Phil's first drawing (*figure 1*)—and what follows are many of the drawings in the order in which they were composed.

After two hours, it looks just like me! In fact, I recognize one of my ears! What he's after is not a reproduced image, obviously, but instead trying to find a way for his hand and eye to apprehend what he—or his hand and eye—imagines is me.

This is the case often with writing, too. But the writer who starts a draft without considering what he or she imagines the subject might be risks missing the subject entirely. It's not possible to know much of anything about your subject when you first begin. So, in the long run, it can be both helpful and also enormously efficient just to noodle at the start of the process.

I mean, when an architect is seized with the idea for a building, he

FIGURE 1

FIGURE 2

doesn't run out into the street and build it. He first mulls, sketches, diagrams, dreams, and mulls some more. He lives with the thrill of the new building, letting the thrill wane and wax and wane and wax, while all the while making plans. Then, he designs the building. Writing can follow the same pathway of creation.

Here's the next drawing (*figure 2*). Now this is better! But, what happened to my head?

No, seriously, this drawing is fascinating. Always, at the beginning of any creative endeavor, it can be hard to see where you're going clearly. Often it's best just to feel around. Just like walking in a strange hallway in the dark, you can paw around for the walls, but not much

FIGURE 3   FIGURE 4

else can be seen or understood.

And yet, this second version is a confident drawing—if you think of drawing as an expression of marks and not exclusively of images. The marks, like my word-palettes, represent the ambition of tackling the unknown. But, not much else. I know that when I write, I often try to work fast. To help keep up the speed, I drop in place-holders to remind me to come back later, giving me time to think through the missing image or scene or metaphor. For instance, I might write "the gray sky VERB GOES HERE over Montana like SIMILE GOES HERE."

The next drawing (*figure 3*) resembles this sort of short-handing method.

It kind of looks like me at least. But it's really just a representation, a place-holder, of me. It doesn't represent the artist's vision of me, just his view. Or, as the Quakers say, Phil is just trying to "get a sense of the meeting." Like a writer in the early sketching phase, he's just trying to understand what he doesn't understand.

I know that many writers worry about what to do with their discards—their failures. Stack them up, is what I say, and push on to the next one. And, always, always, keep your standards high. Working toward and through failure is not lowering your standards. It's the direct opposite. It's raising your standards to the point of inclusion of all effort.

Often when I was modeling for Phil, he and I would talk about our teaching experiences. One of our common experiences is that we both encounter artists and writers, especially beginners, who are certain they know what they want to draw or write. Both of us dismiss this attitude with a crisp "Yeah, right." If you always know what's coming next, why would you bother creating anything in the first place? What the beginning writer or artist needs to discover is that the act of creating unveils our imagination to locate new terrain. And the new terrain is often where the most urgent material lies. In essence, the goal is to seek out the unknowns not the knowns.

As with the next drawing (*figure 4*), looking for the unknowns is

FIGURE 5   FIGURE 6

essential. You can see pretty clearly that Phil is both scrubbing in what he feels about what he's seeing and scrubbing away what his pre-conceived notions might have been. He's drawing with attitude and the result, even this early in the version-ing process, is far from neutral. Just as important, he's working in the moment. What you most need as a writer is the capacity to remain present—to *be here now* when you're writing.

Look closely at the drawing on this page (*figure 5*). You can see that Phil's not drawing from memory. I mean, that's my head. I can see where the eyes might go—or where the eyes were. The story of this one drawing is that Phil can see the shape of my head but doesn't want to commit to the particulars. He's making marks that approximate a figure not trying to explicitly draw a figure. The marks are becoming his subject, not me.

That's how style asserts itself.

Next day, Phil drew the following one (*figure 6*), what I call "Glasses." I'm sure you're thinking, "At last! Here's the finished drawing." Phil had asked me to read to him while he drew—that's why the glasses. Around this time, I began to get a stronger feeling that the model is not a potted plant. I had thought going into the sittings that my role was to, you know, sit. To be still. To be drawn.

But Phil and I spent most of these two-hour sessions gabbing about art, writing, the inner life, our childhoods, women, men, teaching, our kids, politics, and often what it takes to be a creative person in a culture that values monetary and commercial activities as the driving force behind personal success. And most days, too, his wife, Joan, was practicing her drumming in the next room!

I began to get an inkling that what I *said* to Phil during the sitting had an impact on what Phil saw during the sitting. I began to understand that, in a sense, Phil was responding on multiple levels to his subject. Which is to say, he was inventing his subject as much as he was seeing it.

The same holds for writing. You'll always accomplish more when you listen closely to what you're writing. And when I say listen, I mean listen for generative clues that live on the page. For those who don't listen closely, the goal often becomes simply a matter of finishing the drafts. For those who do listen closely, the goal shifts and becomes *listening more closely* to discover what material might be interesting in the next version. It's a form of controlled improvisation.

For instance, if I write "At the blue hour when the birds have started up, I often think of my old aunt who used to hum 'Dixie' and drink iced tea and loved scaring babies," what I can hear in that one sentence is a generative link to writing more about 1) blue hours, 2) old aunt stories, 3) the role of the song "Dixie" in Americana, and 4) sidework for describing how to make iced tea or how to hold a baby, or anything else like this. The more you invent things to make versions that may or may not lead to a poem or story, then the more you discover what must lead to a poem or story.

If what I'm describing is correct, then I have to confess that the next drawing must be what Phil "heard" or "saw" in the previous one called "Glasses" (*figure 6*). What he heard or saw is the drawing I call "Blob" (*figure 7*).

Compare "Glasses" to "Blob," and you might be inclined to think that "Blob' is a major setback. But, again, the method has nothing to do with advancement or improvement. "Blob" isn't a *revision* of "Glasses." It's another version of Phil's take on drawing me. What's at stake has to do with creating another version of whatever impulse dominates any artist's imagi-

FIGURE 7

nation or spirit or mind. The impulse is the thing.

If you think "Blob" is a complete failure, at least compared to "Glasses," then you might be guilty of believing that a writer or artist or creative person gets better every time he or she makes a new piece of writing or art. You'd have thought that Phil's drawings would keep improving. That's the draft-and-revise mentality. But maybe "Glasses" is the *failure*, while the breakthrough for future discovery, at least, occurs in the drawing called "Blob?"

Let me put it another way. Insofar as making art goes, "Blob" demonstrates the futility of only praising perfection and always dismissing imperfection, good versus bad, or success versus failure. But "Blob" also represents the value of simply making *the next thing*, in exploring what there *is* to explore, in following the tributary of the imagination and the passages of invention to arrive nowhere and anywhere. Arrival is not the goal. Making is the goal. By that I mean, *inventing* is the goal.

Whether you make multiple sketches of a scene for your short story or multiple endings, or you just keep re-versioning lines in a poem as in—

1. *The hero spared the ram in the bushes.*

2. *The bushy ram was spare as a hero.*

3. *Spare the ram and the bush for the hero.*

—then you're always learning more about your material and your subject.

Look at the next two drawings (*figures 8 and 9*).

One day Phil and I were talking about the relationship between institutions and artists, a sore subject with Phil. I began to realize that the talk was agitating him, so just to test my theory that the model can have an impact on the artist, I kept up the talk even though I knew it bothered him. Then I said: "How's it going, Phil? You know, I'm not a stump here." You would have thought I called his mother a bear. "It's not working today," he said, putting down his charcoal and looking at me a little suspiciously. And then, as soon as I stood up to come around

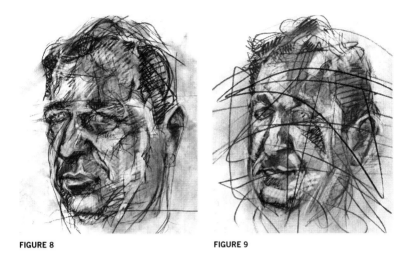

to have a look, he picked up the charcoal again and crossed out the picture—even though, to my eyes, it was one of the more "finished" ones he had made.

The question is often posed: How do you know when a piece is done? It depends on the definition of *know*. I know when a piece is done when I'm ready to move on to the next obsession. If I'm only working toward a final draft, then I've come to the end when I sense that, all things being equal, I have coherence. But, if I'm focused on making versions and not worried about *knowing* if a piece is done, then I can always come back and make another version.

"I want to alter the way I see you," Phil said at the start of the next

FIGURE 10

FIGURE 11

sitting, and proceeded to make the one I call "Insect Eyes" (*figure 10*)
He added: "Most people wouldn't like what I'm going to do, but I've become very interested in this other sort of looking" that involves shapes
rather than lines. After twelve sittings and some 24 hours of drawing,
Phil had decided he knew something about what he was seeing, but he
hadn't yet made the version that revealed it. And he was ready to try
something new.

Next day, he went at it again, aggressively, from a wholly different
attitude. Whatever it was he found out by making the "Insect Eyes"
version freed him to draw from one end of the continuum to another
with confidence. His marks are alive, and his vision of me seems—to

FIGURE 12   FIGURE 13

me, at least—the most intimate. I call the one to the right on the previous page "Intense Face" (*figure 11*). The next day Phil drew the one
above on the left that I call "Wiggle" (*figure 12*).

We were working together at a pretty fast clip at this point in the
summer, and when I came into the studio on the following day, Phil
had put up this formal portrait on a canvas. Compare "Wiggle" to what
I'll call "Portrait" (*figure 13*). By most measurement, "Portrait" would
seem like the success and "Wiggle" the failure. But I want to suggest
it's potentially the other way around. "Portrait" is a less revealing version, even if it is more overtly representational. It's been drawn not
from a live model but from a photograph. In "Portrait," Phil was after a

journalistic style of accessibility. The artifice of "Wiggle," however, says more about the maker than it does the subject.

Now consider the four most recent ones together: "Insect Eyes," "Intense Face," "Wiggle," and "Portrait." What is interesting to me is the nature of the versions: It's not the representation that matters so much, but the *marks* are what matter. I want to say to you that the same issues hold for writing. The writer's imprint comes out in the marks of sentence and syntax, line and stanza, character and scene. Above all, the writer's imprint comes out through the *attitude* revealed in the sentences and syntax, the lines and stanzas, and the characters and scenes. You can see in these four versions that Phil's interpretation of me is the governing force in what we as the audience see. Writers might think of it this way: No one wants a tepid attitude in your *marks*. Write with a fierce attitude—whether it's sentence or scene—and that's what readers will most positively respond to.

These next ones (*figures 14 and 15*) show Phil's comfortable sort of mastery with making my face, for sure. But they also appear quite lifeless.

It was clear to me that, on those days, Phil was tired, a little distracted. That's ok though. They are certainly proficient in their way. But they reveal little about me as a subject and even less about the artist.

FIGURE 14   FIGURE 15

Remember: When you're making versions and not revisions, you give yourself the opportunity to fail more and not consider failing to be fatal. Once you have a version you're committed to as a draft, and you've shifted to revising it toward completion, then you're more interested in working toward your strengths as a writer. That's important, but it's also a *different* topic—perhaps for another book. But, in the versions stages, you can only make the version you can make. Learn from it what you can. Let it help you understand as much about your subject as it will. And then, you know, simply make another one.

7.

In the final three drawings, Phil drew me without looking either at his hand or at the page. He kept his eyes trained only on me—unnerving, I can tell you. His goal was to achieve on the page a kind of visceral, primal interpretation of what he felt he was seeing. It was these final versions, these final interpretations, that Phil felt would most complete the sessions. So he was testing how well he had mastered knowing my face. It's easy to think that the most representational of these nearly two-dozen drawings are the better ones. If the goal of the artist is to report, then, yes, probably they are.

But if the goal of the artist or writer is to represent—that is, re-present as opposed to re-vise—then the issue of better and worse is not essential. Something else is. For me, that something else can be found only through making a sequence of failures—and, by this definition, all of Phil's drawings are failures of a sort (and I suppose they are equally successes of a sort, too). The difference has to do with comparison, with intention, and with finalizing the versions that are most vivid, surprising, and alive.

Have a look at the last three drawings, what I'll call A, B, and C:

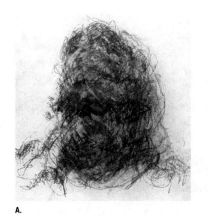

A.

B.

C.

If you had to pick which one was worst, better, and best, I'd say C is the best of these three. To look at C is to see what Phil sees, or rather to see *how* Phil sees. I'd argue, too, that you can see all of the versions expressed inside of C.

Then, suddenly, unexpectedly, after drawing C, after two months of my sitting for him, Phil suggested we stop. In fact, he didn't like C too much in the end. And he hadn't found what he wanted. But he had arrived at a place of interest in the process. C held his interest, I mean, even if it didn't achieve what he hoped it would, or what he saw, as he drew me. Should we pick up again with the drawings some time in the future, I suppose he'll start from a place of greater awareness and knowledge—both of my face and of his faith in his understanding what he's looking for.

And then he'll simply make the next version.

When you look at the next page and see all the versions hung on the wall together (*figure 1*), you can see that he has made, in essence, an entire piece. Viewed like this, you can see how truly interesting all the "failures" are.

On page 87 is a photo of Phil Sylvester with one of his blind drawings of me (*figure 2*). The tape was to keep his hand "on the face." Like Jun Kaneko's image earlier, this photograph reveals a peculiar sort of

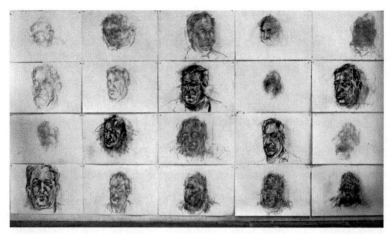

FIGURE 1

self-portrait.

As with writing, the artist isn't actually, or only actually, drawing the subject. Instead, the artist or writer is always composing the versions of what he sees of both the subject and the self. Here's Phil making a similar point to his students before they make their first life drawing:

> *The human figure is an incredibly complex subject. It has many parts, very complex spatial relationships. We have massive amounts of experience, non-drawing experience, with this subject. So we bring a boatload of expectations to the subject. Because we expect so much of our figure drawings and the subject*

itself is so overwhelming, we often have a flinch response before the figure. What I mean by that is, we get so threatened by the demands of this subject that we tense up. We worry that we'll do it wrong so we start worrying about the drawing instead of paying attention to observing.

When a drawing is rushed, one begins to work from memory rather than observation. Our memory of the details of the human figure is nearly nonexistent. We have symbols for the parts, but that is about it. So if you try to make a figure drawing at this stage from memory, you get a sock monkey. You might as well just write the word arm where the arm is, foot where the

foot is, etc., for the amount of observed information you are ac-
tually contributing to the drawing...[So] the first stage is to
gather information. The first stage is often very chaotic. The in-
formation doesn't assemble into any sense at first. As you learn
more and manipulate the information more, order begins to
emerge.

There is a second issue. Drawing the figure or any natural
form for that matter—a blossom, a landscape, an animal—is
like trying to draw a picture of God. It's charming that we would
try. We would learn about God by doing it. And it would reveal
a huge amount about who we are. But good luck. It ain't gonna
capture the true reality of God. What we do as drawers is like
what Dr. Frankenstein was doing. Dr. Frankenstein was creat-
ing a simulation of humans. His first one was horrible, an
abomination to his way of thinking. If he hadn't been such a
baby and quit, his second one would have been better. By his
tenth, he would have had quite a reputation as a monster-mak-
er. By his one thousandth, his monsters would be getting really
good. But no matter how many he made, they would still always
be monsters, not humans. I have the exact same feeling about
my figure drawings. They get better and better, some are genu-

inely beautiful, but every one falls short of the amazing reality of
a living, breathing person.

At one of our first sittings, Phil recommended a book, *A Giacometti Portrait,* by James Lord. The book tells the story of Lord's sitting as a model over eighteen days for Alberto Giacometti to make an oil portrait. What emerges in the book, however, is a portrait not of Lord but of Giacometti. Every time that Lord thinks Giacometti has brought the painting to a satisfying conclusion, Giacometti would—to Lord's exasperation—smear it out during the next sitting and build forward again from that "failed" spot.

Lord reveals that Giacometti has faith that the artist has no choice but to accept that what you are making is almost always different from what you set out to make—or from what is sitting directly in front of you, as in the case of an artist and model, or what is on the page and what you are trying to write, as in the case of a writer and the subject. Here's how Lord describes it:

> *The work had begun to go very badly. Or so he said. He moaned, stamped his foot, exclaimed, "It is abominable!" or "I'm so nervous I could explode!" or "I don't know how to do anything."*

Both Annette [Giacometti's wife] and I tried to persuade him to relax a little or to rest, but without success. However, finally he said, "I don't even know how to hold the brush any more. We'll have to stop."

I stood up. He took the painting from the easel and stood it, as usual, under the light where we could study it from a distance. It was superb. It had never been nearly as good, I thought. The head stood exactly in the axis of the body, which, though still primarily a sketch, had acquired a new tension and solidity. The features were vivid and finely realized, and the likeness, I thought, was excellent, though idealized. So, after all, as I had suspected, it was indeed when the work might seem to him to be at its worst that to the objective observer it might seem best. I told him I thought the painting had never been better. He agreed.

Then I was suddenly overcome with regret at having changed the date of my departure, because I realized perfectly, after sixteen sittings, that without doubt he would paint over the head if he were to work on the picture again. And perhaps it would never afterward be as fine as it was at that moment. In fact, the chances seemed to me slight that it would, for he was not con-

cerned with the painting as a single, objective work to be appreciated as such. That was my concern alone. He would naturally regard the picture almost as a by-product, so to speak, of his endless struggle to portray not merely an individual but reality.

"I'm leaving tomorrow," I said.

"The hell you are!"

"Well, if you ruin the picture now, I'll kill you," I said.

He laughed. "I'll certainly do it all over again from nothing. This is only the beginning. But to have made a start, that's not bad."

Annette and Diego [Giacometti's brother] also agreed that the painting had never before been better.

"Tomorrow we'll see," said Alberto.

Yes, tomorrow, we'll see. Exactly. When he makes the next version. Perhaps you're asking, what's gained by creating this way? What's gained through my repeated lists or Jun's repeated *dangos* or Phil's repeated sketches or Giacometti's repeatedly smearing out one version after another? What's gained with methods based on creating and rejecting and re-creating? What's gained, for a writer, by beginning with language to locate what resonates in experience and not the other way around? What's gained by stringing words together in a sketching phase, half by accident and half by happenstance, by sticking with a subject even when you know it's impossible to achieve perfection? What's gained from resisting the first draft and making failure the goal—by making Frankensteins and not human beings, by rejecting product in favor of realization, by exploring the thousand faces of both self and subject and what you perceive and interpret—or are capable of perceiving and interpreting—at any moment?

For one thing you keep your options open until you find the version that you're most interested in. At my desk, I might write a version and think, "Ah, hell, screw it." Then an hour, a day, a week, or year later I might look at it and think, "Hmm. I'm interested now," and then make another version. Either way, one version is no more essential than another. But all the versions are essential to the organism of each other. They suggest possibilities for future compositions just the same as they accomplish something on their own. More important, what they enable for me as the writer is a journey toward clarity about what I perceive I'm making. That's why I believe every writer has a thousand faces. Which is to say, every subject that you write about has a thousand faces, too.

Working in this method lets you keep your emotional investment invested in the method and not in the draft or the revision. I say to myself, "They're just versions anyway!" So I keep hanging my versions on the wall, so to speak, just like those drawings. I don't know what they are, I don't know what they'll lead to, and I don't know what I know about them. I don't know, I don't know, I don't know. I'm writing what I don't know and it's leading me to what I do know.

Therefore: I make another one. Another version. Another face. Now I have two, now I have ten. Now I have a thousand. In the past, I had my one draft, revising it and revising it, risking turning a 10 into a 2. That's awesome. So long as it works, that's beautiful. It's tried and true. But now I focus on my method—which is a method and not a poem—and I stack up my versions which might be poems and which might not be poems. My writing a single poem, as I've experienced it, is so much further along when I first start to *compose* because I know so much more about the potential poem when I begin to write it—that is, I'm very late in the process of discovery when I finally commit to what can only be called the first draft. Then again, at the same time, every time I begin with what I know, in each subsequent version, I must reckon with the reality of what I don't know. So the process is re-actualized over and over again.

Through making versions and not drafts I learn to trust the accident. Given my background in sports, I think of it this way: I train, I prepare, I work hard, and I focus on what I can focus on. I never know what's going to happen and the act of creation becomes more alive—at least, for me. And I stick with it. Once I get to that "first draft," of course, I work on revising it in the traditional manner. And, well, revising your writing from first draft to completion is a topic, as I say, for another book. For now, avoiding the first draft is a good first step. Try that.

Finally, there's some essential gratitude required, too. After Giacometti says, "We'll see tomorrow," it's obvious that he will, in the end, destroy the one he's "finished" and make another version the next time. "We'll see," he says. Meaning, *we'll see it differently tomorrow*.

The rest of the Lord-Giacometti sitting reveals the suffering and gratitude Giacometti feels about his work and also his relationship to his subject:

> *Then he went into the bedroom to lie down, for he felt a pain in his chest. He had said, when I told him that I would stay the two extra days, that we must celebrate, so I followed him into his room and fixed myself a Scotch and water. We talked for some time. Suddenly Alberto sat up in the bed and began to sing very*

loudly, "I am cured!" Annette hugged and kissed him. He said he wanted to go to the café to eat something. We all three went over there. I sat with them for a time.

"Tomorrow," I said, "you'll be walking a tightrope" But I felt that it was I in a way who would actually be on the tightrope, because, having once seen how beautiful the painting could be, I felt desperately anxious that it should not ultimately remain less so. And yet I was powerless to affect its final state. Or was I? I began to wonder.

"Oh, tightropes," he said, shrugging. "I've got plenty of those."

As I left he called after me, "Thank you, thank you for everything."

8.

All along in this book I've been describing *my* method. But I want to say again, it's certainly and by no means the only or even best method. It's what has worked for me. I may continue to use it, or I may veer off in another direction. Try it out. It might be helpful to you in some way. Or maybe not—and that's ok.

Still, I do feel strongly that developing a method is useful, especially if the method has a threshold for success that's continuously affirming. As I've been saying, failure in writing is just fine—it's generative. But you don't want a method that makes you feel like a failure. Instead, you want a method that catalyzes you to fail into success. I mean, I make lists of words. How can I go wrong with that?

A Pulitzer Prize-winning novelist once described to me his bout with developing a writing method, and his experience is instructive. He said that at one point in his career he felt his writing process was too inconsistent. Some days he wrote well, other days not so well, some days sporadically well and other days sporadically not well. He couldn't get into a groove or find a consistent wavelength.

So he decided he would write 1,000 words a day. It didn't take long before he began to feel that he was a failure even at that. Not because he wasn't writing or even writing well, but because he seldom reached the 1,000 word plateau. His goal was a 1,000 words but there were many, many days when he only got to 850 or 950 or 500. On the days when he didn't reach his goal, his method made him feel terrible. No matter what he actually wrote, he felt like a fraud.

Next he opted for writing steadily for four hours a day. Again, some days he met the goal, other days he didn't. But on the days when he didn't, he felt wretched, even when he wrote for three-and-a-half hours. It didn't matter. Four hours was the goal, not three and a half. Something must be wrong with him. Couldn't he get another half hour in? I mean, it's just another half hour. So he'd feel terrible.

The result of this negative reinforcement led him sometimes to doubt his focus and to question his commitment as a writer. Then, in the funk of self-doubt, he'd sometimes just stop writing altogether.

I hope this hasn't happened to you. Because, face it, when you add up day after day of two, three, or three-and-a-half hours of writing (even as opposed to four, four, and four hours a day which was your goal), it still amounts to a decent accumulation of writing. But he couldn't see it. It's too bad.

I've encountered a lot of writers over the years who get hung up on their failure to meet these sorts of quantitative goals and then they give up writing. A good method continually brings you back to the page at the pace that works in your life.

As for that Pulitzer Prize-winning novelist, he finally arrived at an elegant method that works for him. He abandoned word counts and he abandoned hourly progress. Instead, he decided that his writing method was simply *to be at his writing desk for two hours a day*. Whether he wrote a word or not, as long as he was in the place where writing takes place, he was achieving his method.

Some days he'd write a little, read the paper, surf the Web. Other days, he'd fill two hours entirely with writing. Still other days, he'd stare out the window. All of it, however, contributed to his method—which was simply to be present so that he could be able to write. Over time, the ratios would change. At the beginning, he'd fritter the two hours and write barely anything. But once he had a story that seized his imagination, he'd write more and fritter less. Two hours became three. Three became four. And then, over time, viola! A novel.

I love this approach. As long as you can get to your desk and chair, it's nearly fool proof. For you, it might not be two hours. It might be 20 minutes twice a day. It might be two-and-a-half hours every other day. It might be 45 minutes every morning. It might be six hours a day. Whatever works in your life, try that. The only requirement is to sit down in one place for a prescribed amount of time. My guess is, eventually, you'll get restless with so much sitting and then, just to break the inertia, you'll begin to peck out a few sentences, then a few more, then a few more. But even if you don't, when the kitchen timer goes off and you've reached 20 minutes or two hours or whatever, you can chalk it up as a good day for writing. You can evaluate what's actually on the page another time—but at least you'll likely have something to evaluate.

That's an excellent method for just getting into a place to write.

Let me list some other methods I've heard of that might help you get to that sit-down place. Any one of these, or any combination of these, might help you. The important thing is to discover a method that works *for you* and then keep at it. You can always discard it for another one later, a different method that better suits your creative aims. Here are twenty-five starter ideas. Consider that most of these might last about 5–20 minutes. Make sure you give your method a few months' effort in order to see if it works for you or not.

1. *Call your mother, sibling, or a friend, and talk for fifteen minutes. Then begin writing.*

2. *Leaf through a photo album or a coffee table art book or read from a writer you love. Then pick one thing to describe from that resource, and write toward that. Then throw it out.*

3. *Listen closely to music. It doesn't matter whether the song is a Bach concerto, Bob Dylan's acoustic takes, or a pump-you-up sports chant. Then get to writing.*

4. *Draw for ten to twenty minutes. Then write.*

5. *Lie on the floor for five minutes with your eyes closed and remember something essential from your life. Then describe what you're remembering. This is especially good if you tend to remember the same essential things. Write different versions of those memories. Hang onto these!*

6. *Take a walk, get a cup of coffee, and walk home very slowly.*

7. *My favorite: stare out the window.*

8. *Start with side work. Take a line from a poem you're working on or a character from a story and write 25 more lines based on that line or 500 words based on the character. Put that scribbling aside (it might come in*

handy later).

9. *Copy down a poem you love. Same goes for a passage of prose. I recommend doing this by hand. There's a wonderful synaptic release that happens when you do this, as if you can trick yourself into believing that you are William Faulkner writing those beautiful sentences—and it feels good to "write" so well, doesn't it?*

10. *Imitate a writer you love for 500 words—aiming for coloring that writer's style and diction. Throw it out.*

11. *Thumb through some of your works-in-progress quickly and make copy-editing changes. Put that down. This is a good way just to get your mind flexible. But remember, composing and editing can't be done at the same time. When you compose, aim for "failure." When you edit, aim for clarity.*

12. *Make a word-palette from words discovered at random from a dictionary. Simply thumb through a dictionary, writing down the first word you notice. Make it totally arbitrary. Then use all the words in a piece of nonsense. Put that scribbling aside (it might be of use later—really, it might!)*

13. *Sketch in first person for three months. Then switch to third for three months. And any other variation of these in terms of point of view, present or past tense, or tone (as in write angry for three months, then write sentimentally for three months). Then write.*

14. *Sketch a dream. Throw it out. Then write.*

15. *Sketch a secret. Throw it out. Then write.*

16. *Write a letter. Mail it. Then write.*

17. *Raise your temperature. Run, jump, or skip. Writing takes energy.*

18. *Begin by tinkering with failed pieces—not to fix them so much as to tune up your mind, to elevate your imagination into the zone of creativity.*

19. *Or, try the opposite. Begin by circling the best parts of your writing—a fine word choice, a strong sentence. Give yourself a break. There are plenty of times when you write quite well. Take notice. Then compete with your best.*

20. *Write 100 words of the silliest nonsense. Throw it out. Then write another 100 words of something else silly. It's a way to burn the fat.*

21. *Nothing wrong with sketching an outline. W. B. Yeats did all*

the time.

22. *Wash the dishes. This is the Agatha Christie method.*

23. *Make a new version of the weakest part of the poem or story you've been working on. Don't throw it out! This one might actually come in handy.*

24. *Switch the machine. If you write by hand, type a version of something first instead as a warm up. If you type out your versions, start by hand. If you use a Number #2 pencil, switch to a mechanical pencil. If you use a Bic pen, switch to a Cross pen.*

25. *Create a pet character—a dog that can talk, a favorite auntie, anything—and begin every writing experience by writing a random monologue in the voice of this character. Then get to work.*

Finally, one method to use before writing anything is simply to spend time getting organized. Spend time mulling and thinking, taking an inventory of what you know and what you don't know about a subject.

The other day, for instance, I ran into my friend, Floyd, who told me was working on an essay about *The King and I*. He'd been in a stage production as a boy and the whole experience meant a lot to him. But he didn't want to just launch into writing about it. Instead, he read a biography of Anna Leonowens, the real life "Anna," as well as her memoirs. He re-read Margaret Landon's 1944 novel, *Anna and the King of Siam*. He read as much as he could find about Rogers and Hammerstein's writing and production of the 1951 Broadway play, *The King and I*, which is based on the novel. And, of course, he watched the classic Walter Lang musical, starring Yul Brynner and Deborah Kerr. And he'd seen several staged versions over the years.

He set out, he told me, intent on writing something about his relationship to *The King and I*. But, in the process, after all the thinking and preparing and mulling and research, after taking inventory of what he knew and didn't know, he found himself writing not about *The King and I*, but about his mother.

That's a great example of how a disciplined method—in Floyd's case, taking time to do diligent groundwork—can steer you into an essential discovery about your imagination and your subject. By taking time to prepare to write a first draft, he discovered more about his subject and about the unconscious connections inspired by his subject, before he ever began to write.

That's another example of what I mean when I say that every writer has a thousand faces. At the beginning of this book I described Joseph Campbell's characterization of the hero. The hero, like the writer, receives a call out of the ordinary world. Reluctant at first, the hero receives encouragement and crosses the threshold into the fullness of the imagination where he encounters tests, assistants, and challenges. The hero endures a variety of ordeals, then seizes on that experience and pursues transformation of the experience. Finally, the hero returns to the ordinary world with the treasure of knowledge.

Creating a method for your writing—a method that you repeat with discipline and interest—is the symbolic act of creating the conditions for you to be called out of the ordinary world into writing in the first place. To write is to enter a consciousness that is separate from the everyday. To write means to enter a magical realm of imagination and invention and discovery in which you become aware of the thousand faces that you inhabit, that inhabit you, that you encounter, and that you work to transform from experience into literary art.

9.

So there are a couple dozen or so ideas for creating a method for writing. Take what works for you or create variations and leave the rest for someone else. Just because you work in one method doesn't mean it'll be your method for life. Find the method that will suffice.

Even beyond devising a method, I know all too well that just writing alone is troubling business. And, I know, I know, the Alberto Giacometti angst of it all can be overwhelming.

But consider this, beyond developing a method—after the difficulties, after the false starts, after the solitude and turning away from friends and family ("no, I can't make it for dinner, I need to get some writing done"), after the doubts and the foggy hunches of what you want to write, after the little tatters of rejection slips litter your desk, and even after successes and specific triumphs ("yes, that is the right adjective!"), after staring at the wall or staring out the window, after the certainty of feeling it's all pointless—there's still that first question posed by Adrienne Rich that might never go away: What is it that you need to keep going for the long haul? And do you want to?

I've been talking about getting to the first draft. I suppose you've been wondering, "Ok, I'm with you. Avoid the first draft! Now what?" Well, write. There's no other way to get it done.

In writing this book, I've imagined that you've been writing for some time or you used to write but haven't for a bit, or you dearly want to write, have been promising yourself for years and years that you would write. And of course, I suspect that you do want to write for the long haul. You're still reading this because you want to keep the long-haul fires going. You *must* keep the fires going. You take workshops in order to remain accountable to your own aspirations—even an uninspiring workshop is good enough for that. And I have been assuring you that actual failure is better than risking failure. Well, for me, it's better. I can say that much. I construct, build, compose, and fashion my lists of words—my pile of discards—into what could actually be a poem. I'm driven to play in the medium of poetry—words and silence—more so than to write poems. If I focus on one, the other is inevitable.

So here's the thing: One's initial sense of ambition as a writer naturally gives way to time, and what you realize is, it isn't mere ambition to be a writer that matters. You realize that what is driving you all this time is compulsiveness. So you build narratives that come out of the recurring seasons of life and memory and projection. You sketch poems in the voice of King Philip V of Spain. You chalk out screenplays about growing up on a commune and becoming a stockbroker. You write and write and write and have no idea what it is you're making or whether it's any good. And whether you publish any of this or not, the same impulse always exists: *to write*. It's what calls you to the page. It's what makes you feel poorly when you haven't been writing in a while. It's one of the things that define you personally as a human being—inside of yourself, your inner self, and your sense of being a writer. Or a painter. A sculptor. A parent. It's one of the thousand faces you wear to make a record of having lived.

This compulsion won't go away. You have the opportunity while you're alive to respond to it. Question is: What will you do? I believe that writing and living a creative life requires two things, ambition and discipline. Trust this fact: Before you wrote your latest poem, story, or essay, it never existed before in the history of time or the history of humanity. Never existed. Until you made it.

What I'm getting at is, don't make your writing or your method or your art-making such a precious thing. Your finished story or poem or your painting, choreography, or sculpture may have some preciousness in it. But the drafts or versions, whatever, no.

Creativity of all kinds must include a workbench in an oil-stained garage. It's a construction site with a hand-made sign that says, "No architects allowed!" It's labor. It's toughing it out. It's tilling the soil. And while you're down on your knees tilling the soil in the garden of your creative life, down on your knees praying to the gods to give you a break, to confer upon you immortality, to strike you, say, with the best words in the best order, you know, I suggest you pick a few weeds while you're down there. I suspect that the gods see your writing like playing the lottery, anyway. They're willing to confer their powers upon you, but you have at least to meet them half way and buy a ticket. Write what you know or write what you don't know and then, either way, you'll know what to write.

No one can tell you how to write, and surely I can't. But, here's the deal, I can tell you this: Your writing is right there for you to do and no one can keep you from doing it. It's right there. In front of you, right now. In the lived moments of your daily life. In the remembered fragments of your dreams. In the insistent fabric of your good and lousy memories. In the wafts of what you can invent from your imagination. In the raw medium of words in any language. In the facts and objects in your home and the environment outside your window. And God knows where else. Nowhere else. Everywhere else. It is, as Adrienne Rich suggested, a long haul. But a worthy one.

Sometimes the greatest understanding about the process of writing comes from forgetting everything you think you know. It comes by allowing a few things to remain mysterious. But, every time, the greatest understanding about the process of writing comes from your actual method of composing and writing.

DAVID BIESPIEL is the founder and director of the Attic: A Haven for Writers. His books include *The Book of Men and Women*, *Wild Civility*, *Pilgrims & Beggars*, and *Shattering Air*.

LaVergne, TN USA
18 January 2011
213034LV00005B/42/P